for 1000+ tutorials ... use our
free site .... drawinghowtodraw.com

DRAWING FOR KiDS

HOW TO DRAW WORD CARTOONS WITH LETTERS & NUMBERS

WORD FUN & CARTOONING FOR CHILDREN BY TURNING WORDS INTO CARTOONS

JUST CHILLING DUCKY

5.

↓ NOW YOU TRY ↓

LOVELY SPIRAL ROSE

1. r

2.

3.

4.

5.

6.

7.

↓ NOW YOU TRY ↓

CUTESY LITTLE GIRL

1. girl

2. girl
Letter S Shaped Curve
Letter J Shape

3. girl

4. Draw Letter W Shape over the Letter i Shape

5. Letter S Shapes

6.

Letter S
Shapes

↓ NOW YOU TRY ↓

ENERGETIC LITTLE BOY

1. boy

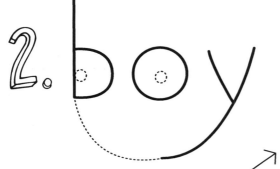

2. boy

Letter M Shaped Zig-Zags

3.

4.

PEPPY LITTLE DOGGY

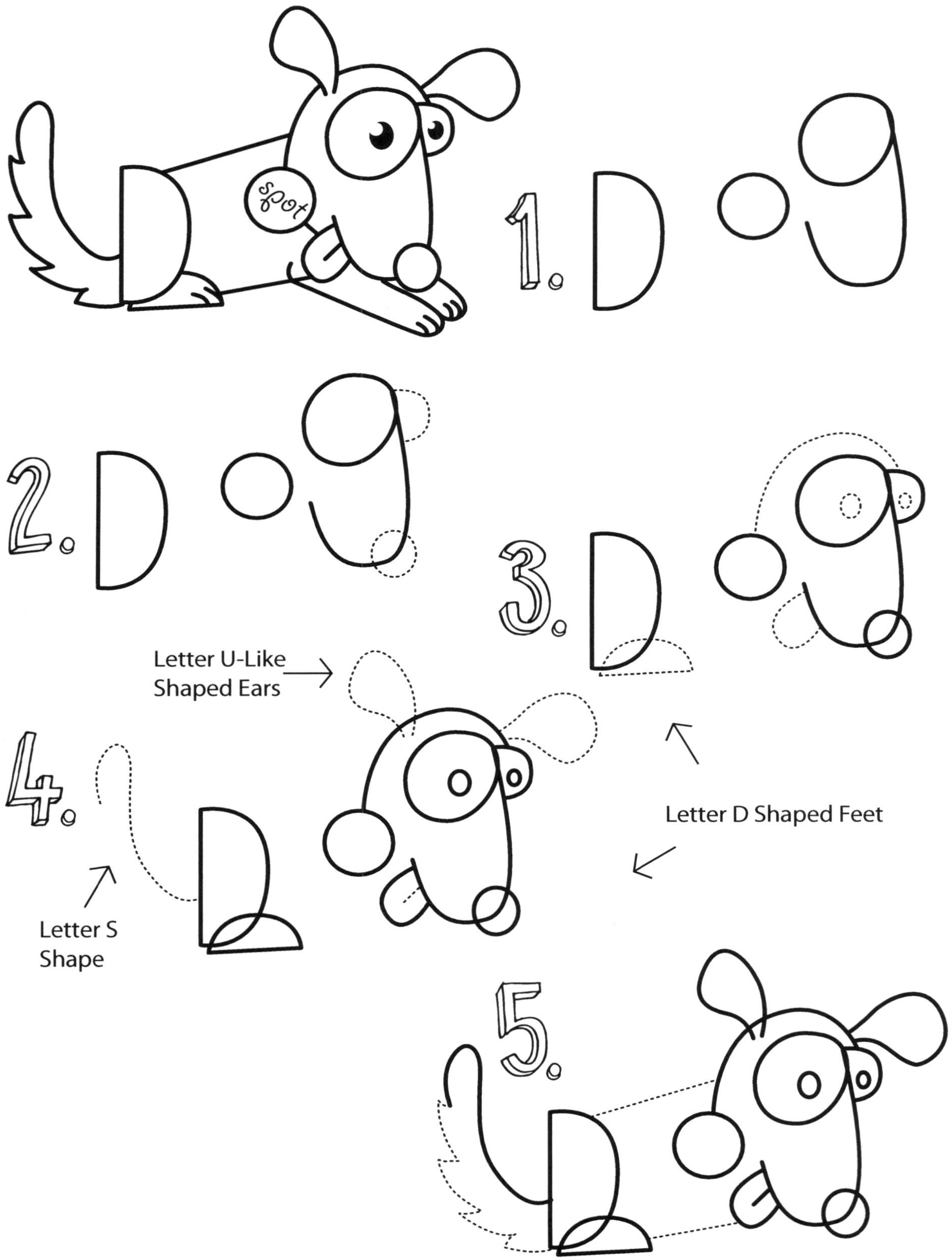

1. D

2. D

3. D

Letter U-Like
Shaped Ears →

Letter D Shaped Feet

4.

← Letter S
Shape

5.

6.

#3 Shape

7.

spot

↓ NOW YOU TRY ↓

FUZZY LITTLE KITTY

1. cat

2. cat

3. cat

← ?-Shape

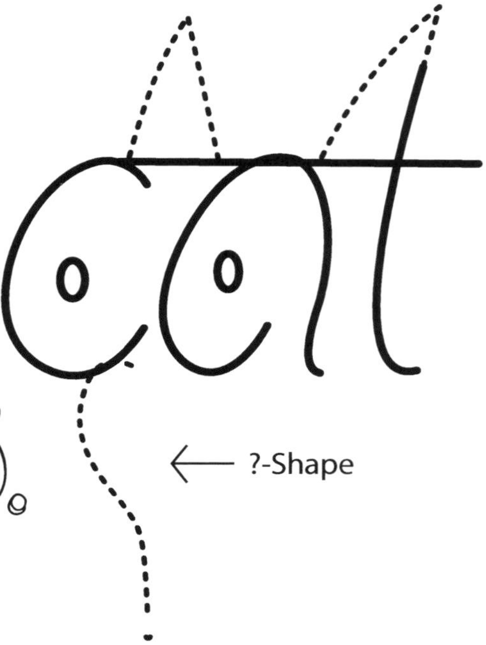

4. cat

#11 and Letter C →

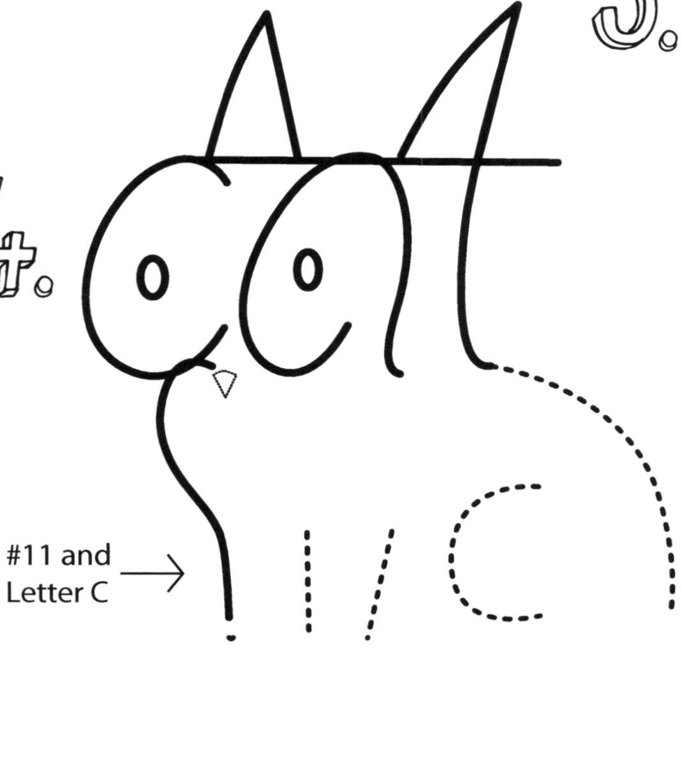

PEACEFUL SAILBOAT

1. Letter B Shape

2. Letter O Shape

3. Letter A Shapes

4. Now the Letter T Shape

5. Letter S Shape

6.

7.

NOW YOU TRY

MOO-MOO COW

1.

2.

3.

4.

5.

6.

⬇ NOW YOU TRY ⬇

PLAYFUL DEER

1.

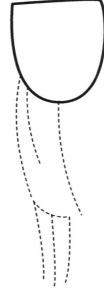

2.

3.

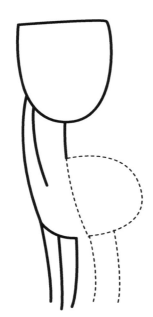

4.

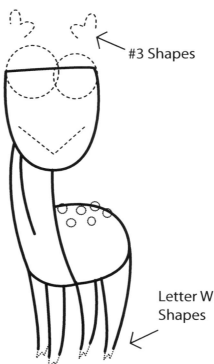

#3 Shapes

Letter W
Shapes

5.

Letter e Shapes

Letter J Shape

NOW YOU TRY

CHEESY MOUSE

1.

2.

3.

4.

Letter M Shape

SLEEPY TEDDY BEAR

1.

2.

3.

4.

5.

6.

NOW YOU TRY

FESTIVE ELF

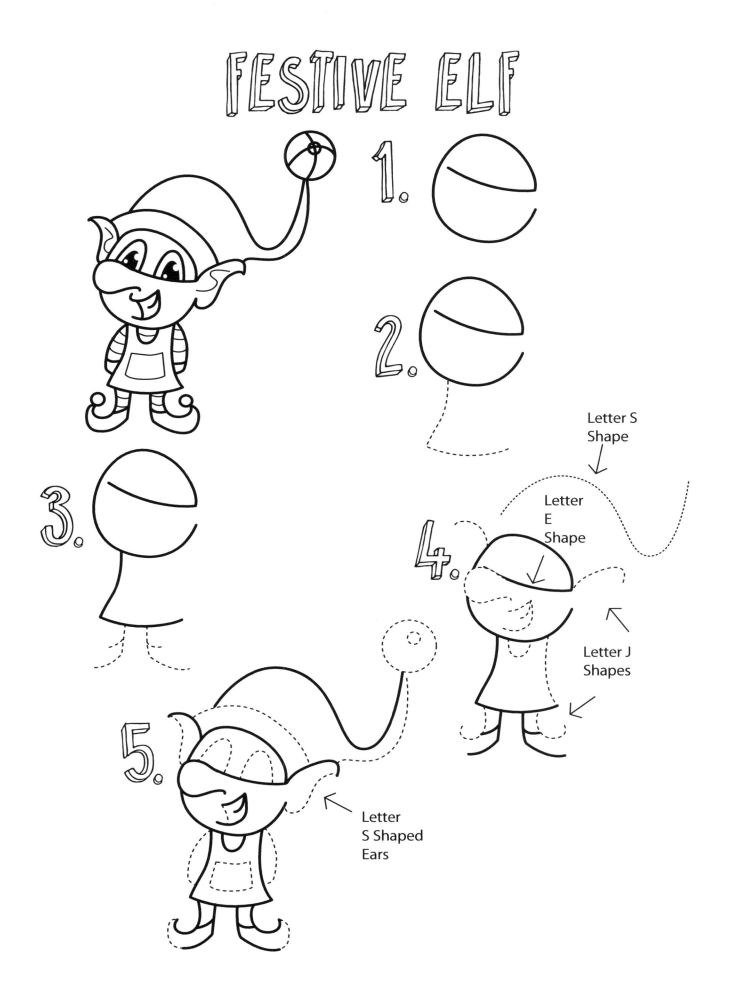

1.

2.

Letter S
Shape

3.

Letter
E
Shape

4.

Letter J
Shapes

5.

Letter
S Shaped
Ears

6.

7.

NOW
YOU
TRY

BUGGY CAR

1.

2.

3.

4.

5.

6.

↓ NOW YOU TRY ↓

NESTY BIRDY

4.

↓ NOW YOU TRY ↓

SLOPPY PIGGY

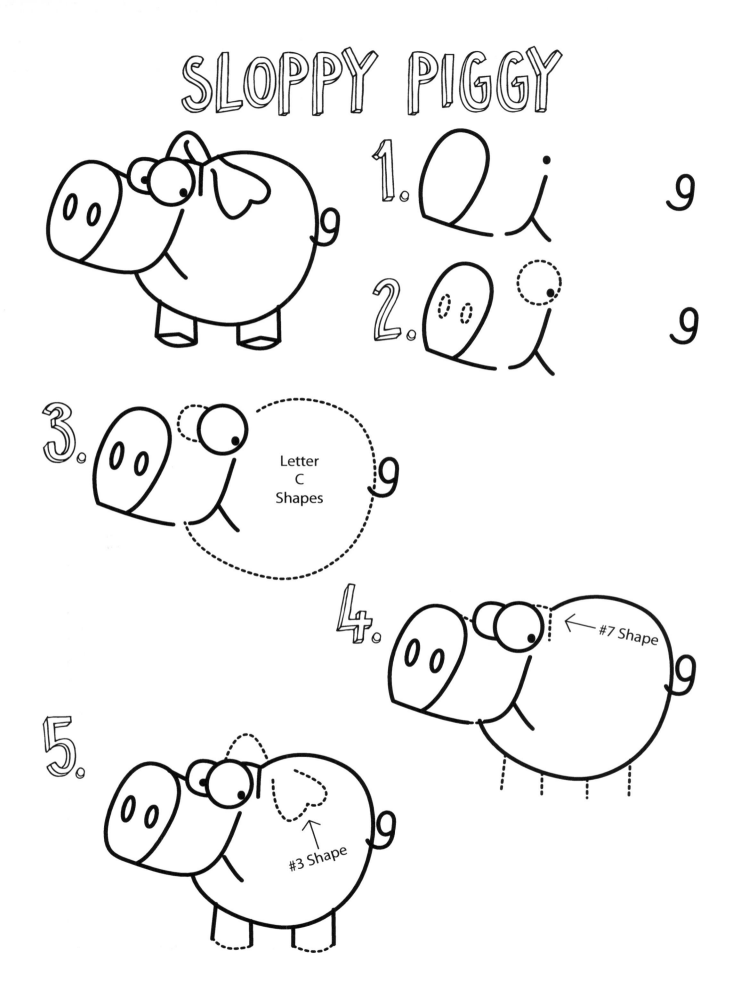

1.

2.

3. Letter C Shapes

4. ← #7 Shape

5. #3 Shape ↑

SWIMMY FISHY

1. 2.

3.

4.

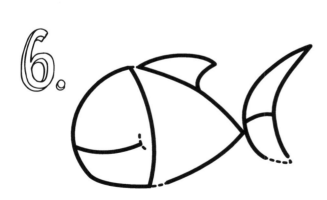

5.

6.

7.

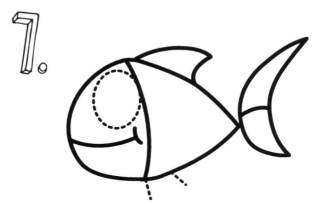

8.

9.

↓ NOW YOU TRY ↓

PRETTY LADY

1.

2.

3.

Letter M
Shape

4.

5.

⬇ NOW YOU TRY ⬇

SOPHISTICATED MAN

1. 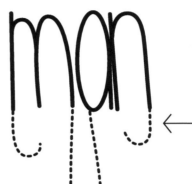 man

2. man ← Letter J & U Shapes

3.

Wavy Letter M-Like Shape

4.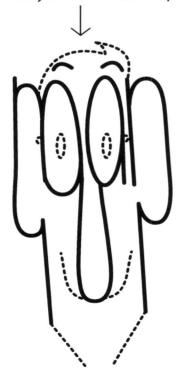

5.

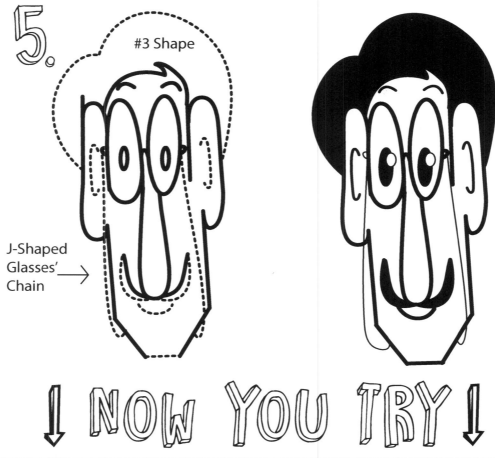

#3 Shape

J-Shaped
Glasses'
Chain →

↓ NOW YOU TRY ↓

HOOTY OWL

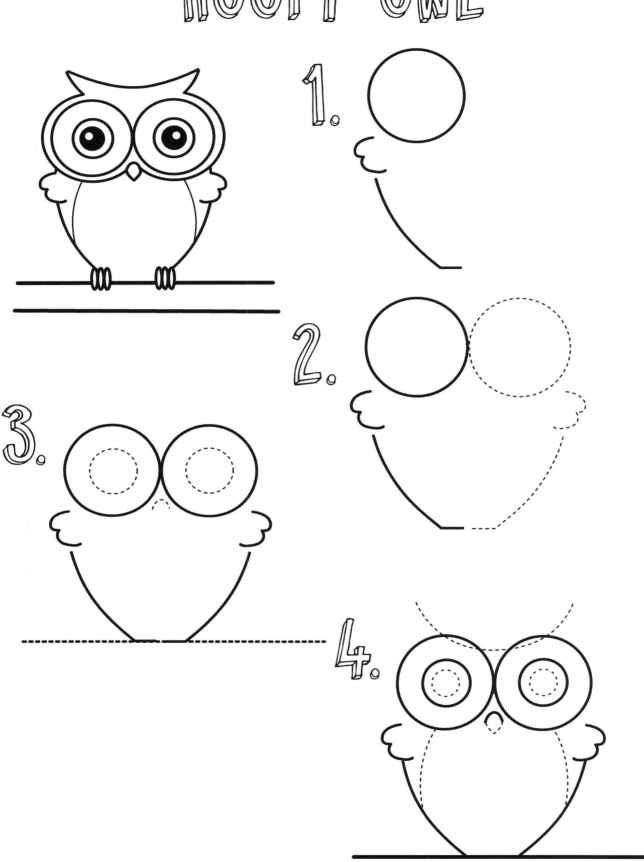

1.

2.

3.

4.

5.

6.

NOW YOU TRY

FOXY FOX

1.

2.

3.

4.

5.

?-Shaped Tail

W Shape

?-Shaped Tail

6.

↓ NOW YOU TRY ↓

MOXIE OX

1.

2.

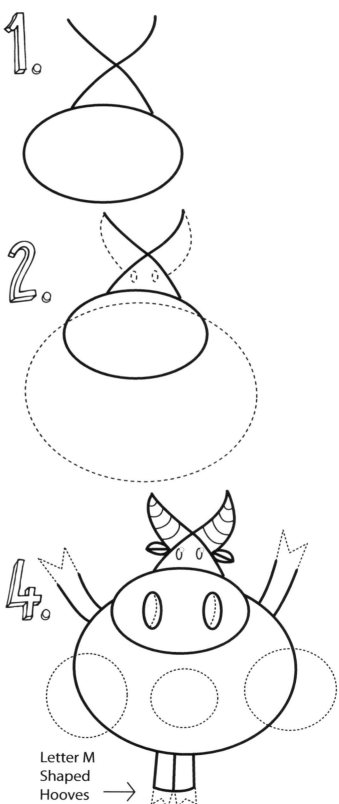

3.

Letter E
Shaped
Ears

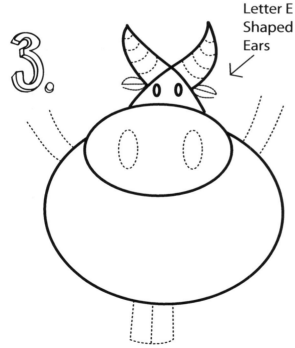

4.

Letter M
Shaped
Hooves →

5.

↓ NOW YOU TRY ↓

FLYING BUGGY

1.

2.

3.

4.

5.

Letter Z
Legs

6.

NOW YOU TRY

CREEPING ANT

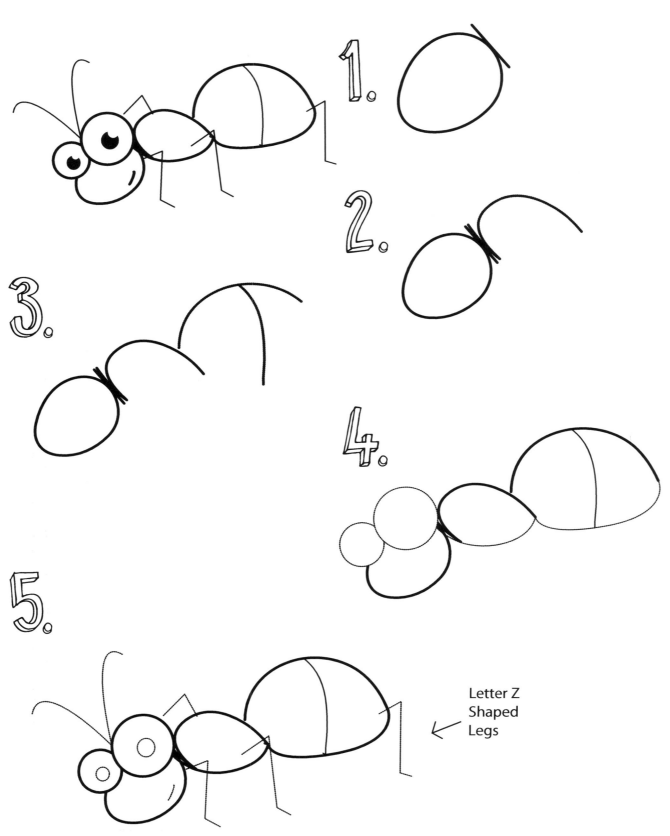

1.

2.

3.

4.

5.

Letter Z
Shaped
Legs

6.

↓ NOW YOU TRY ↓

GENTLE LION

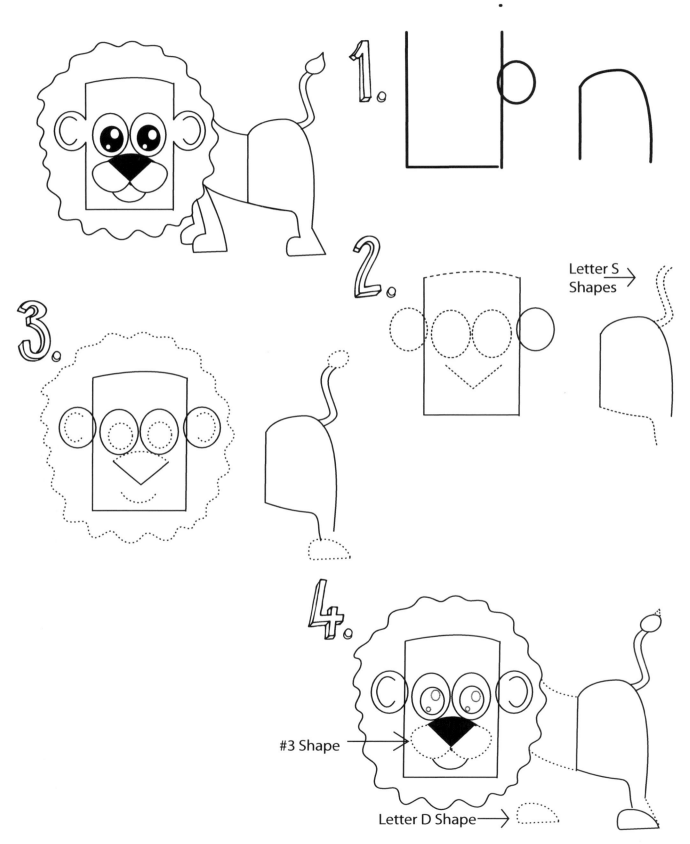

1.

2. Letter S Shapes →

3.

4. #3 Shape → Letter D Shape →

5.

? - Shape

⬇ NOW YOU TRY ⬇

BOSSY KING

4.

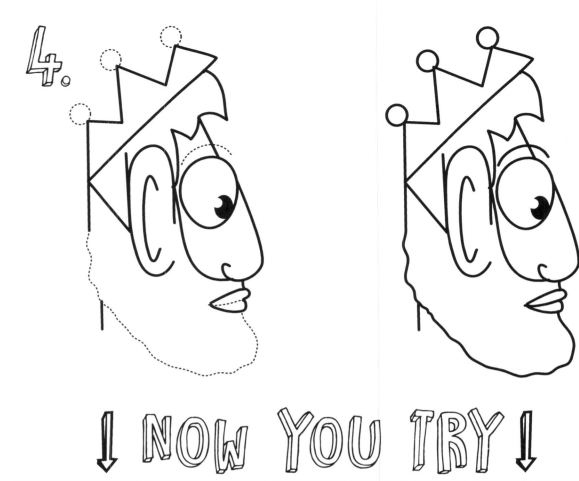

NOW YOU TRY

COOKY CHEF

1.

2.

3.

4.

OUR OTHER BOOKS

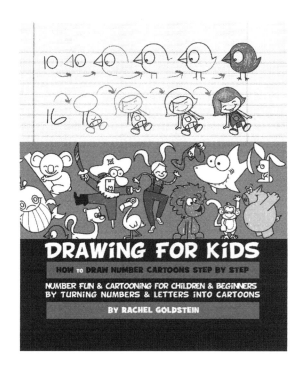

Please Give Us Good Reviews on Amazon!
If You Give us a 5 Star Review, and Email us
About it, We Will Do a Tutorial Per Your
Child's Request and Post it On
DrawingHowToDraw.com

12710801R00033

Made in the USA
San Bernardino, CA
11 December 2018